RESTORE

Dr. Larry Green Sr., Ed.D., Ph.D.

Copyright © 2024 by Dr. Larry Green Sr., Ed.D., Ph.D.

Cover Design Copyright © 2024 by T. Fielding-Lowe Media Company

All rights reserved.

"Parts of this book are based on a true story. In order to protect the privacy of individuals, some names and identifying details have been changed."

Although the author and publisher have made every effort to ensure that the information in this book was correct at press time, the author and publisher do not assume and hereby disclaim any liability to any party for any loss, damage, or disruption caused by errors or omissions, whether such errors or omissions result from negligence, accident, or any other cause.

No part of this book may be reproduced, stored in a retrieval system, or transmitted in any form or by any means, electronic, mechanical, photocopying, recording, or otherwise, without the prior written permission of the author, except as provided by USA copyright law.

ISBN: 979-8-9985703-7-7

Printed in the United States of America

T. Fielding-Lowe Company, Publisher

https://www.tfieldinglowecompany.com

DEDICATION

With profound gratitude and deep affection, "Restore" is dedicated to the cherished memories of Alexander and Lillie P. Clanton, beloved parents, as well as to Betty, a devoted wife, and Larry, Darryl (Samantha), and Jessica (Dashawn), cherished children. Each has been a source of pride, contributing to a beautiful family tapestry. It is encouraged to remain united and resist any attempts by the world to unravel these bonds, striving to embody the great men and women of God intended to be.

Profound thanks are given to a praying mother whose belief in higher education was unwavering. Her encouragement, "If God teaches others, He will teach you too. Remember, it's not about what's on your head, but what's in your head," often accompanied by playful references to my a "AFRO," continues to resonate even though she cannot witness the ultimate academic success. Her lasting legacy remains a profound inspiration.

To Betty, gratitude is expressed for your godly presence, prayers, love, and unwavering support over the past forty-nine years, which have been a driving force during challenging times.

To my granddaughter Jordan, it is remarkable how someone so small can make such a significant impact with fond memories of requests to visit and go to the park. To Lilyana, the joy of playing hide-and-seek games and being called "Poppy" is treasured. To Samai, the joy and laughter you bring into the room are deeply appreciated, ensuring the name "Green" lives on. Lastly, Aurora, who has woven into the heart and Spirit of the family, is celebrated for being uniquely herself and encouraged to achieve all things through Christ who strengthens her.

My deepest gratitude is also extended to Thea Fielding-Lowe, the esteemed publisher, whose unwavering support and guidance have been crucial in bringing this book to fruition. The expertise, dedication, and belief in this project have been invaluable, and the collaborative effort is profoundly appreciated.

FOREWORD

In the face of a world marked by violence, systemic injustice, and persistent trauma, particularly within African American communities, the theme of restoration becomes not only timely but necessary. In recent decades, the African American community has continued to experience the devastating effects of violence in multiple forms—personal, communal, and institutional. From gun violence and domestic abuse to police brutality and the ongoing impact of historical racism, African Americans have often been caught in a cycle of deep-seated trauma, which extends not only across individuals but also within families and neighborhoods.

Such trauma, unresolved and unattended, weakens the moral, spiritual, and emotional fabric of individuals, impairing their ability to experience peace and wholeness. Yet, in the midst of these broken realities, Dr. Larry Green comes to remind us that the church remains a beacon of hope and healing, specifically through the leadership of African American pastors who are deeply committed to the work of restoration.

Dr. Green's concept of "restore" evokes the biblical idea of renewal and redemption, a central theme in Christian theology. As David pleaded in Psalm 51:12, "Restore to me the joy of Your salvation and uphold me with a willing spirit," the prayer for restoration is a recognition of both personal and communal brokenness, coupled with an appeal to God's transformative power. In African American churches, which have historically served as sanctuaries in times of crisis, this prayer for restoration finds resonance. African American pastors have played pivotal roles in guiding their congregations through the dark valleys of oppression, offering not only spiritual guidance but also practical support. In the face of today's traumas, Dr Green suggests that they are uniquely positioned to address the emotional and psychological wounds inflicted by violence.

A powerful tool for addressing these wounds is found in nouthetic counseling, a biblical counseling approach grounded in the principles of Scripture. Nouthetic counseling—derived from the Greek word "noutheteo," which means to admonish, warn, or counsel—seeks to confront sin, bring about repentance, and offer hope for change through the transformative power of God's Word. Unlike secular approaches to trauma counseling, which may focus primarily on psychological theories and coping mechanisms, nouthetic counseling is deeply concerned with the spiritual condition of the counselee. It asserts that at the heart of many emotional and psychological struggles is the issue of sin, whether personal or environmental, and that true restoration comes when individuals are realigned with God's will for their lives.

For African American pastors leading nouthetic counseling within their communities, the work of restoration is particularly challenging but profoundly rewarding. Many of these pastors serve in urban environments where violence is not a distant abstraction but a daily reality. Whether dealing with the aftermath of police violence, gang-related crime, or domestic abuse, these leaders must navigate a complex emotional landscape, where fear, grief, anger, and despair often dominate. They must address not only the immediate emotional trauma but also the larger cultural and systemic factors that contribute to this violence.

Here, in Restore, Dr. Green offers a lens into the nouthetic counseling framework by providing a biblically grounded path forward. Trauma induced by violence often leads to questions of justice, fairness, and the presence of God in the midst of suffering. African American pastors are well-versed in this spiritual wrestling, often drawing from the rich theological resources of the Black church tradition, which has long connected suffering with the hope of redemption. Nouthetic counseling allows pastors to affirm the gravity of the trauma while pointing their congregants toward the hope of restoration that is found in Christ. The promise is that while sin and violence have marred the world, God's redemptive work is ongoing and that healing, though not always immediate, is assured through faith and obedience to God's Word.

Equally important, nouthetic counseling presents the opportunity to bring the community into the process of restoration. In African American culture, the church has always been more than a place of worship; it has been a center of social and communal life, where individuals find support, encouragement, and accountability. Nouthetic counseling is not an isolated, private process but one that happens within the context of a caring and committed community. African American pastors, aware of the collective nature of both trauma and healing, often incorporate communal elements into their counseling ministries.

The Word of God offers the ultimate path to healing and peace, and through nouthetic counseling, I believe like Dr. Green that pastors can help their communities rediscover that path, one heart at a time.

Come within Restore learn that restoration is not merely about the absence of trauma but about the presence of God's redemptive power at work in the lives of individuals and communities. It is about reclaiming what has been broken, and trusting that through God's grace, even the most devastated hearts can be made whole once again.

Reverend Professor Keith Magee, Th.D.
Global Pastor and Professor of Social Policy
London, England

TABLE OF CONTENTS

Foreword
by Reverend Professor Keith Magee, Th.D. i

Introduction 1

Chapter 1: A Cry for Change: From Tragedy to Transformation 4

Chapter 2: Urban Violence 9
    Overcrowded Housing
    Poor Education
    Lack of Economic Employment
    Gang Violence

Chapter 3: Trauma 13
    How Trauma Can Manifest

Chapter 4: The Role of African American Pastors in Community and Counseling 17
    Historical Context and Evolution of African American Churches
    The Role of African American Pastors Today
    Pastoral Counseling and Mental Health Support
    Addressing Community Issues
    Challenges and Opportunities
    Restoration through Nouthetic Counseling

Chapter 5: Guiding Hearts: The Crucial Role of Pastors in Counseling and Community Support 25
    Counseling and Psychotherapy
    Cultural Understanding
    Pastoral Counseling

Chapter 6: Value of Spiritual or Religious Coping 30

Chapter 7: Nouthetic Counseling 35
    Biblically Based
    Education and Training
    Critique of Nouthetic Counseling
    Benefits for Trauma Survivors

Final Thoughts 44

Bibliography iv

About the Author xi

Introduction

The Church has long stood as a beacon of hope, resilience, and transformation in the rich tapestry of African American history and culture. As an institution deeply embedded in the struggle for freedom and equality, it has been a sanctuary for spiritual renewal and a catalyst for social change. The role of African American pastors, as illuminated in this profound work, reflects this tradition of unwavering dedication and multifaceted service.

This book offers a compelling exploration of the essential roles that African American pastors play in community and counseling contexts. It deftly navigates the historical journey of African American churches—from their beginnings as clandestine places of worship during the era of slavery to their evolution into powerful centers of social advocacy and spiritual guidance. These churches have provided a space for worship and served as crucial hubs for education, social justice, and community empowerment.

The chapters thoughtfully address the complex and vital roles that African American pastors fulfill today. Beyond their spiritual leadership, they act as counselors, educators, and advocates, addressing a spectrum of issues that range from individual mental health challenges to broader community concerns. This book highlights how these pastors integrate nouthetic counseling—a biblically rooted approach focused on sin, repentance, and spiritual transformation—into their pastoral care. This approach, deeply connected to their congregations' cultural and religious fabric, offers a holistic pathway to restoration and healing.

What stands out in this work is the seamless blend of faith and activism that characterizes the ministry of African American pastors. Their role extends beyond the pulpit, as they actively engage in community leadership and advocacy, addressing systemic issues such as economic inequality and social justice. This dual focus on spiritual guidance and community empowerment reflects African American churches' enduring legacy as both spiritual sanctuaries and agents of social change.

This book also candidly explores the challenges African American pastors face in contemporary ministry. Balancing spiritual responsibilities with administrative duties, financial management, and personal self-care presents a complex array of demands. However, despite these challenges, pastors remain steadfast in their commitment to their congregations and communities. They adapt to the evolving landscape of religious practice and community needs, ensuring their ministries remain relevant and impactful.

The relevance of this book is born out of the need to do something different to meet the needs of the community where I am on assignment from the Lord. After exhaustively searching for literature, I did not find any studies involving the use of a nouthetic method with urban pastors dealing with the trauma of urban violence. The uniqueness of this book is rooted in my belief that nouthetic counseling is an effective tool for urban pastors to use when ministering to those impacted by violence.

Through the lens of nouthetic counseling, this book articulates a framework for restoration deeply rooted in faith and biblical principles. The RESTORE framework—Recognize, Examine, Support, Teach, Openness, Restore, and Empower—serves as a guide for pastoral care, offering a comprehensive approach to addressing spiritual, emotional, and relational needs. This framework underscores the transformative power of faith in fostering personal and communal growth, resilience, and unity.

Nouthetic counseling, as prescribed by Jay Adams (2009), is a method of counseling thoroughly grounded in scripture. It may be effective for crisis counseling and for counseling clients who are disproportionately affected by trauma associated with urban violence. "Restore" aims to investigate the art of nouthetic counseling and explore how we, as a church, pastor, or Christian counselor, can help and support urban communities suffering from violence to heal from the trauma they endure.

In closing, this work is a testament to the enduring significance of African American pastors in nurturing spiritual and social well-being. Their contributions are not merely historical but are vibrant and evolving, reflecting a commitment to justice, empowerment, and healing. As you delve into the pages of this book, may you gain a deeper appreciation for the profound impact of African American pastors and their vital role in shaping spiritually enriched and socially empowered communities.

Chapter 1: A Cry for Change: From Tragedy to Transformation

The deaths of Marcus, Tasha, and Amara caused an uproar within Norfolk County. Anger and sorrow spilled into the streets as the community demanded action. People gathered in protest, their voices echoing through the city, calling for leaders to step up and make meaningful changes. They demanded that the police focus on making arrests and solving crimes instead of harassing innocent residents.

Community leaders held meetings, urging the city council to address the root causes of violence and invest in programs for the youth. They called for increased funding for education, mental health services, and job training to offer alternatives to the dangerous paths that had claimed so many lives.

As pressure mounted, the police department was forced to reevaluate its tactics. Officers began to engage more with the community, building trust and working collaboratively to solve crimes. Investigations into gang activity intensified, leading to several key arrests and a reduction in street violence.

The loss was an unbearable burden for the families of Marcus, Tasha, and Amara. Marcus's parents, Mike and Janice James, who had pinned their hopes on his bright future, were left with a void that no accolades or memorials could fill. Each day was a struggle as they faced the haunting absence of their son, their home filled with reminders of what could have been.

Marcus's family had always encouraged him to be his very best, instilling in him the belief that excellence in all he did would open doors to a brighter future. They often reminded him that good grades would pave the way to college, leading to a well-paying job that could lift the entire family out of poverty. Their hopes were tied to his success, and Marcus did not disappoint—he was a shining star in academics, earning numerous awards that lined the walls of their modest home. His achievements were not just a source of pride but a beacon of hope for a better tomorrow. Those awards, once symbols of his potential, were painful reminders of a future that would never come to pass.

Tasha's mother, Candida, already familiar with the harsh realities of their neighborhood, found herself drowning in grief and regret. She grappled with the pain of losing her daughter to the very violence from which she had tried to shield her. The nights were the hardest, as memories of Tasha's laughter and dreams played endlessly in her mind.

Regina, Amara's mother, could barely function, her heart shattered by the senseless loss of her innocent child. The sound of children playing outside her window constantly reminded her of the joy she would never experience again.

Regina went from being active at her church, participating in the adult mass choir and helping with local missions, to barely attending Sunday services. She met with her pastor a couple of times but was left with the same questioning position: Why? The community's support was a small comfort, but nothing could ease the agony of knowing her baby girl was gone forever.

The loss of Marcus, Tasha, and Amara became a turning point for Norfolk County, changing the community's mentality. The tragedy sparked a movement that sought to reclaim the city from the grip of violence and create a safer, more hopeful future for all its residents.

As a pastor with over 40 years of experience in urban ministry, I know that many people today seek out their pastors as a primary resource in times of crisis. In our community, the pastor is not just a figurehead; they are a trusted source of help and solace. People know that when they turn to their pastor, they will receive encouragement and support without judgment. In these moments of darkness and despair, the light of faith and compassion shines brightest, offering hope and healing to those who need it most.

Within African American communities there are a plethora of reasons why parishioners and community members seek out pastors for help with mental health issues. Family breakdown in our community bleeds into our churches, schools, and the tender lives that form the generations we are raising. If we do not address the root cause, we will face a future filled with violence and senseless deaths.

A high-crime area refers to communities with crime ratios higher than the overall state-weighted average for two consecutive years. The role of a pastor and educator in a high-crime area is profoundly impactful. The experience of counseling and performing funeral services for those affected by violent deaths is undoubtedly challenging but also a unique opportunity to minister to individuals in their time of greatest need.

The responses they have observed—either turning towards the Church and faith or turning away from them—highlight the complex and deeply personal nature of grief and loss. For those who seek refuge in their faith, the Church becomes a sanctuary and a source of comfort, helping them navigate their pain. However, the challenge is more significant for those who feel abandoned and angry as they grapple with a crisis of faith on top of their grief.

In these situations, the role of a compassionate and understanding pastor is crucial. A pastor offering a listening ear, a non-judgmental presence, and a message of hope and love can make a significant difference.

Here are a few ways pastors might continue to offer support throughout both responses to grief:

1. For Those Turning to Faith

- Encouragement and Support: Continue to offer spiritual support and encouragement, reinforcing their faith and providing them with resources like scripture readings, prayer groups, and faith-based counseling.
- Community Building: Foster a sense of community within the Church, where individuals can find mutual support and understanding from others who have faced similar losses.

2. For Those Turning Away

- Non-Judgmental Listening: Provide a safe space to express their anger, doubts, and feelings of abandonment without fear of judgment.
- Gentle Engagement: Share messages of God's unconditional love and the idea that having questions and doubts is okay. Sometimes, sharing your own experiences or those of others who have struggled with faith can be reassuring.
- Practical Support: Offer practical assistance, such as helping with funeral arrangements or connecting them with community resources, which can demonstrate the Church's care beyond spiritual matters.

The work of a pastor is vital in bringing solace and hope to a community that faces such profound challenges. By continuing to be a steady, compassionate presence, pastors can help individuals find their way through their grief, whether turning towards faith or grappling with their feelings towards it.

Not a day goes by that I do not hear some devastating news regarding a young person being either a participant or victim in an act of violence. Just this past Saturday, I was asked to preach at a funeral service for a young man who was shot to death at the age of 22. This is just another incident that has fueled my passion to become more effective in nouthetic counseling. The Lord has commissioned me to pastor people who live in a community that is no stranger to violence.

Chapter 2: Urban Violence

Many scholars, academia, and other researchers have addressed the problem of violence. For example, in her article "Urban Violence: War by any Other Name," Amy Serafin (2014) addressed many reasons that contribute to urban violence, such as overcrowded housing, poor education, and the lack of economic employment. In his 2003 article, Vigil asserted, "To broaden and deepen the picture, many other factors need to be considered, such as ecological, socioeconomic, sociocultural, and socio-psychological" (p. 225). In addition to these three contributions to urban violence, I also believe gang violence is another critical factor that contributes to urban violence. Let's look closely at all four factors and how they contribute to urban violence.

Overcrowded Housing

Overcrowded housing can contribute to urban violence in several ways. Firstly, it can lead to increased tension and conflict among residents forced to live in close quarters, often with limited privacy and resources. This heightened stress can escalate into disputes and violence, especially in neighborhoods where economic and social pressures are already high.

Additionally, overcrowded housing may be associated with poverty and lack of opportunity, factors that are often linked to higher crime rates. When individuals and families struggle to make ends meet in cramped living conditions, they may feel more desperate and resort to illegal activities as a means of survival or to alleviate financial strain.

Moreover, overcrowding can exacerbate social issues such as gang activity and drug trafficking. Tight living spaces can make it easier for criminal elements to operate covertly and exploit vulnerable individuals within the community.

Addressing overcrowded housing is essential for improving living conditions and quality of life and reducing the underlying social and economic factors contributing to urban violence.

Poor Education

Poor education significantly contributes to the increase in urban violence for several reasons. First, it limits opportunities for young people in areas with inadequate educational resources. This lack of academic and personal development opportunities can lead to frustration, hopelessness, and disengagement from mainstream society, potentially pushing individuals towards criminal activities as an alternative path. Second, poor education is often associated with poverty, a significant risk factor for involvement in crime. Without access to quality education and the skills needed for stable employment, individuals may find themselves trapped in a cycle of poverty, increasing the likelihood of resorting to crime as a means of survival or advancement. Additionally, education is crucial for developing critical thinking, problem-solving, and conflict-resolution skills. Without these skills, individuals may struggle to navigate complex social situations or handle conflicts peacefully, leading to violence as a default response to challenges or disagreements.

Moreover, in communities with poor educational opportunities, young people are more vulnerable to recruitment by gangs or other criminal organizations. These groups may exploit disenfranchised youth by offering a sense of belonging, identity, and financial incentives that are lacking elsewhere, perpetuating cycles of violence within communities. Third, and last,, poor education perpetuates social inequality by limiting access to opportunities for social mobility. When specific population segments are systematically denied access to quality education, the gap between the haves and the have-nots widens, fostering resentment, social unrest, and sometimes violence.

Addressing urban violence requires addressing its root causes, and improving educational opportunities for residents of urban areas is a crucial step in breaking the cycle of violence and fostering safer, more equitable communities.

Lack of Economic Employment

Urban violence and lack of employment are interconnected in several ways. Economic disadvantage and desperation often characterize areas with high unemployment rates, making individuals feel desperate to provide for themselves and their families, which can result in increased participation in criminal activities for survival or economic advancement. Employment provides social and economic mobility opportunities, but without access to stable employment, individuals may feel trapped in cycles of poverty and hopelessness. This can lead to feelings of frustration and resentment, potentially resulting in violent behavior.

Additionally, a lack of legitimate employment opportunities can make individuals more susceptible to gang recruitment or involvement in criminal networks. These groups may offer financial incentives, a sense of belonging, and protection in exchange for participation in illegal activities, thereby perpetuating cycles of violence within communities. Unemployment also leads to psychological and emotional stress, including feelings of inadequacy, worthlessness, and depression, which can exacerbate existing tensions within communities and contribute to interpersonal conflicts and violence.

High levels of unemployment can disrupt the social fabric of communities, leading to social isolation, breakdown of family structures, and weakening of community bonds. This breakdown in social cohesion can create environments where violence is more likely to occur, as individuals may lack the social support networks necessary to resolve conflicts peacefully. Studies have shown correlations between unemployment rates and crime rates, with periods of economic downturn often associated with increased violent crime. When individuals are unable to find employment, they may turn to illegal activities as a means of financial support, leading to higher levels of urban violence.

Addressing the root causes of unemployment, such as lack of access to education, economic opportunities, and support services, is essential for reducing urban violence and creating safer, more resilient communities. By investing in job creation, skills development, and social support programs, societies can help break the cycle of poverty and violence and promote positive outcomes for individuals and communities.

Gang Violence

Another factor is the rise of gang violence. As you have read before, gang violence can increase when there is overcrowded housing, poor education, and a lack of economic employment.

One important factor contributing to closing the gap between aggressive behaviors by males and females may be increased gang activities among females. R.L.To Maginnis (1995), in his analysis of youth gangs, stated that because youth gangs account for a disproportionate share of youth violence, their potential for contributing to a future crime wave is enormous. Maginnis later reported that a survey carried out by Metropolitan Life Foundation in

2000 on schools and gang violence showed that more than half (57%) of law enforcement and one-third (34%) of students and teachers said that gang or group membership was a significant cause of violence in schools in the United States (Solis, 2009, p. 53).

Chapter 3: Trauma

Trauma is an emotional response to a deeply distressing or disturbing event that overwhelms an individual's ability to cope, causes feelings of helplessness, diminishes their sense of self, and limits their ability to feel a full range of emotions and experiences. Trauma can manifest in various ways, including changes in personality and behavior. Individuals may exhibit increased irritability, anxiety, or depression and may withdraw from social interactions or activities they previously enjoyed. They might struggle with intrusive thoughts or memories and experience physical symptoms such as insomnia or fatigue. Understanding the complex interplay between trauma and behavior is essential for providing practical support and interventions.

How Trauma Can Manifest

In the case of Regina, the mother who lost her child Amara, the scenario illustrates how trauma can manifest in various behavioral changes, impacting emotional, spiritual, and physical well-being. Regina's loss triggered a cascade of symptoms consistent with post-traumatic stress disorder (PTSD) and depression, disrupting her previous vibrant and engaged demeanor.

Hyperarousal and hypervigilance may be evident in Regina's sensitivity to her surroundings, as she remained on edge, anticipating potential threats or reminders of her trauma. This state of alertness can be exhausting and overwhelming, further exacerbating her emotional distress. Additionally, Regina's avoidance of activities she once enjoyed, such as singing in the church choir and teaching Sunday school, reflects a common coping mechanism used by trauma survivors to shield themselves from distressing memories or triggers associated with their trauma. Regina may have felt temporary relief by withdrawing from these activities, but ultimately, this avoidance could impede her ability to find joy and meaning in life.

Re-experiencing the trauma through intrusive thoughts, flashbacks, or nightmares could further disrupt Regina's emotional equilibrium, causing her to relive the pain and anguish of her son's loss as if it were happening anew. These distressing symptoms might intrude upon her daily life, impairing her ability to function effectively and exacerbating her feelings of helplessness and despair.

Emotional dysregulation was evident in Regina's struggle to manage her emotions, as evidenced by her difficulty sleeping and loss of appetite. Trauma can disrupt the brain's ability to regulate emotions, leading to mood swings, irritability, and emotional numbness. Regina might oscillate between periods of intense sadness, anger, and detachment, making it challenging for her to maintain stable relationships and cope with the demands of daily life.

Self-destructive behaviors, such as substance abuse or self-harm, may emerge as Regina attempts to cope with overwhelming emotions or numb her pain. These maladaptive coping strategies provide temporary relief but can exacerbate her suffering and increase her vulnerability to further harm. Furthermore, Regina's trust in others may be shattered by her traumatic experience, particularly if she feels betrayed or abandoned by those she once relied on for support. This erosion of trust can isolate her from potential sources of help and hinder her ability to seek the assistance she needs to heal and recover.

Finally, Regina's social withdrawal reflects her desire to shield herself from potential judgment or rejection as she struggles to navigate the complexities of her grief and trauma. However, isolation can heighten her feelings of loneliness and despair, increasing her sense of alienation and disconnection from others. Trauma can profoundly impact behavior, as illustrated by Regina's experience in the aftermath of urban violence. Regina's story helps us better understand the complexities of trauma and behavior and the types of support and interventions necessary to help survivors heal and rebuild their lives.

Chapter 4: The Role of African American Pastors in Community and Counseling

In the fabric of African American life, the Church is more than just a religious institution; it is a vital community hub where individuals find spiritual fulfillment and essential support for life's challenges. This dynamic is deeply rooted in the community's historical journey, where churches have often been the focal point for social cohesion, education, and empowerment. From the days of slavery to the civil rights movement and beyond, African American churches have served as places of refuge and resilience, fostering a sense of identity and solidarity among their congregants.

Historical Context and Evolution of African American Churches

The history of African American churches in the United States is intricately woven with the struggle for freedom, equality, and social justice. During slavery, churches provided enslaved individuals with spaces to worship, commune, and organize in secret, away from the oppressive gaze of their masters. These early congregations nurtured spiritual growth and became bastions of resistance and resilience, where members shared messages of liberation and hope through spirituals and sermons.

Following emancipation, African American churches expanded their roles as community centers, providing education, social services, and political organizing platforms. Leaders emerged from within these churches who played pivotal roles in advancing civil rights and challenging systemic racism. Figures like Martin Luther King Jr., a Baptist minister, exemplified the intersection of faith and activism, using the pulpit to galvanize communities against segregation and injustice.

The Role of African American Pastors Today

Today, African American pastors play multifaceted roles within their communities, serving as spiritual leaders, counselors, educators, and advocates for social change. The trust and respect they command stem from their deep understanding of the historical and cultural contexts in which their congregants live. This understanding allows pastors to address spiritual needs and their communities' complex social, economic, and psychological challenges.

Pastoral Counseling and Mental Health Support

One of the most critical roles of African American pastors is providing mental health support within their congregations. Many African Americans view mental health through a holistic lens that integrates spiritual, emotional, and physical well-being. This perspective often leads individuals to seek guidance from pastors who are seen as not only spiritual guides but also trusted counselors who understand their cultural and religious backgrounds.

Nouthetic counseling, a form of pastoral counseling rooted in scripture and characterized by a focus on sin, repentance, and biblical guidance, plays a significant role in the counseling practices of African American pastors. Drawing from biblical principles and their deep understanding of cultural nuances, pastors offer nouthetic counseling to address issues such as marital conflicts, substance abuse, grief, and trauma within their congregations. This approach emphasizes personal responsibility, spiritual growth, and reconciliation with God and others.

Historically, African Americans have faced barriers to accessing quality mental health care due to systemic racism, stigma, and distrust of mainstream medical institutions. Pastors fill this gap by offering pastoral counseling that is culturally sensitive and grounded in faith traditions. They provide a safe space where congregants can explore their mental health challenges without fear of judgment or misunderstanding, incorporating prayer, scripture, and spiritual practices into therapeutic interventions.

Addressing Community Issues

Beyond individual counseling, African American pastors are pivotal in addressing broader community issues such as economic inequality, educational disparities, and social justice. Churches under their leadership often serve as community centers that host educational programs, job training initiatives, health fairs, and legal clinics. Pastors collaborate with local organizations and government agencies to advocate for policies that promote equity and justice, leveraging their moral authority and community influence for systemic change.

In addition to counselors, African American pastors serve as community leaders and advocates. They tackle complex issues such as historical trauma and cultural identity within their congregations, drawing on their understanding of societal influences and diverse worldviews (Sue & Sue, 2011). Beyond spiritual guidance, they actively engage in efforts to combat violence, promote healing, and advocate for social justice in their communities (Walsh, 2008).

Spirituality and religious affiliation serve as potent bonds in urban African American communities, transcending differences in race, culture, and gender (Shafranske & Malony, 1996). This communal strength is evident in African American pastors' multifaceted roles as mentors, teachers, mediators, and moral guides who embody and reinforce the values of their communities (Boyd-Franklin & Walker Lockwood, 1999; Mattis, 2002).

Challenges and Opportunities

Despite the invaluable contributions of African American pastors, they face challenges in navigating the complexities of modern-day ministry. The duties of pastoral care, community leadership, and advocacy demand pastors balance spiritual responsibilities with administrative tasks, financial management, and personal self-care. Many pastors operate within resource-constrained environments where community programs and social services funding may be limited.

Moreover, the evolving landscape of religious practice and community engagement presents challenges and opportunities for African American churches and their pastors. Changes in societal norms, technological advancements, and generational shifts influence how churches connect with younger congregants and address contemporary social issues. Pastors must adapt their ministry approaches to remain relevant and responsive to the evolving needs of their congregations and communities.

Restoration through Nouthetic Counseling

Nouthetic counseling, rooted in biblical principles and characterized by a focus on sin, repentance, and spiritual transformation, plays a pivotal role in the pastoral care provided by African American pastors. Within the context of African American communities, where spirituality and faith are foundational, nouthetic counseling offers a pathway towards restoration and healing. Pastors who engage in nouthetic counseling follow four steps to ensure restoration.

Step 1: Acknowledgment and Repentance

Central to nouthetic counseling is acknowledging personal responsibility for one's actions and attitudes. African American pastors guide individuals through introspection and repentance, helping them confront sinful behaviors and attitudes that may hinder their spiritual and emotional well-being. This step fosters accountability and encourages individuals to seek forgiveness from God and reconciliation with others.

Step 2: Biblical Guidance and Transformation

Drawing from Scripture, African American pastors provide biblical guidance and practical wisdom to address life's challenges. Nouthetic counseling emphasizes the transformative power of God's Word in renewing the mind and heart. Pastors offer scriptural insights and principles that promote spiritual growth, resilience, and emotional healing within their congregations.

Step 3: Healing and Reconciliation

Nouthetic counseling creates a safe space within the church community where individuals can experience healing and restoration. African American pastors facilitate conversations that promote forgiveness, reconciliation, and healing from past hurts and traumas. Individuals are encouraged to seek emotional healing and restored relationships through prayer, pastoral guidance, and supportive community networks.

Step 4: Integration into Community and Service

As individuals experience restoration through nouthetic counseling, African American pastors encourage them to integrate into the church community as active participants and servants. Nouthetic counseling emphasizes the importance of using one's restored life and testimony to serve others and glorify God. Pastors support individuals in identifying their spiritual gifts and talents, empowering them to contribute positively to their communities and advocate for justice and equity.

Incorporating nouthetic counseling into their pastoral care practices, African American pastors offer a holistic approach to restoration that addresses spiritual, emotional, and relational needs within their congregations. Through the transformative power of faith, biblical guidance, and community support, nouthetic counseling provides a pathway for individuals to experience healing, reconciliation, and renewed purpose.

The process of nouthetic counseling can be encapsulated in the acronym "RESTORE":

Recognize: Pastors help individuals recognize their spiritual, emotional, and relational struggles within the context of biblical truth.
Examine: They encourage individuals to examine their thoughts, feelings, and behaviors in light of God's Word and identify areas that need restoration.
Support: Pastors provide emotional and spiritual support, walking alongside individuals through their journey of healing and reconciliation.
Teach: They teach biblical principles and truths that offer guidance and direction for living a restored life in Christ.
Openness: Encouraging openness and vulnerability, pastors create a safe space for individuals to share their struggles and receive godly counsel.
Restore: Ultimately, the goal is restoration—restoring individuals to spiritual wholeness, emotional well-being, and healthy relationships through God's transformative grace and truth.
Empower: Lastly, pastors empower individuals to live out their restored identity in Christ, equipping them to walk confidently in faith and purpose.

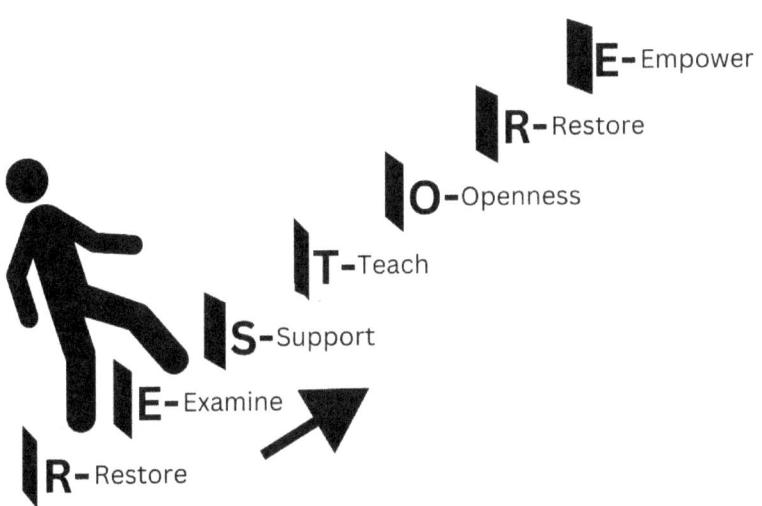

Through the RESTORE framework of nouthetic counseling, African American pastors facilitate profound personal and spiritual growth, fostering resilience, unity, and community empowerment. The role of African American pastors in community and counseling is rooted in a rich tradition of faith, resilience, and social activism. By incorporating nouthetic counseling into their pastoral care practices, pastors offer a holistic approach to restoration that addresses spiritual, emotional, and relational needs within their congregations. Through the transformative power of faith, biblical guidance, and community support, nouthetic counseling provides a pathway for individuals to experience healing, reconciliation, and renewed purpose. As custodians of a profound legacy of faith and social justice, African American pastors navigate the challenges of modern-day ministry with unwavering commitment and compassion. They uphold the transformative power of faith in overcoming adversity and building inclusive communities where all individuals have the opportunity to thrive. African American pastors remain steadfast in their role as advocates for justice, mentors for youth, and stewards of cultural heritage, ensuring that the legacy of the Black Church as a sanctuary for spiritual renewal and social empowerment endures for generations to come.

Chapter 5: Guiding Hearts: The Crucial Role of Pastors in Counseling and Community Support

Most people, when facing emotional or mental challenges, typically seek help from professionals like psychologists or psychiatrists (Kreger, 2011). Each person brings unique burdens, wounds, and life experiences, often influenced by their cultural backgrounds. This diversity underscores the importance of counseling, which encompasses varied specialized fields such as marriage and family counseling, academic and career guidance, mental health support, substance abuse recovery, and pastoral counseling. Despite their differences in approaches and techniques, these fields share a common goal: assisting individuals in finding solutions to their challenges and improving their overall well-being.

Counseling and Psychotherapy
Counseling and psychotherapy represent broad spectrums of philosophies and methodologies tailored to meet the diverse needs of clients. Psychiatrists specialize in addressing severe mental health issues and have the authority to prescribe medications, whereas psychologists and counselors focus on therapeutic interventions that do not involve medication (Schimelphening, 2011). The decision-making process around medication can sometimes lead to challenges and complexities in treatment, highlighting the nuanced nature of mental health care delivery.

A significant distinction between psychotherapy and counseling lies in the treatment duration and practitioners' qualifications. . Counseling typically involves short-term, goal-oriented sessions to promptly address specific issues (Schimelphening, 2011). In contrast, psychotherapy often entails more extended, in-depth explorations of psychological issues conducted under the guidance of a psychotherapist (Patrick, 2010). Psychotherapists, with their academic grounding in psychology, employ various theoretical frameworks such as psychodynamic, behavioral, humanistic, or social psychological theories to aid clients in achieving mental well-being and personal growth (Patrick, 2010).

Despite the effectiveness of secular approaches to counseling and psychotherapy, some individuals seek guidance that integrates spiritual and moral dimensions into their healing process. This is where pastoral counseling serves a unique role, distinguished by its foundation in religious teachings and values. Unlike secular counseling, which may overlook spiritual aspects of a person's life, pastoral counseling provides a perspective that acknowledges and integrates these dimensions. For many individuals, especially within religious communities, this approach offers a profound sense of comfort, guidance, and moral clarity.

Cultural Understanding

Pastors, deeply rooted in their communities, possess a level of accessibility and cultural understanding often unmatched by mental health professionals who may not share the same cultural or spiritual background (Mattis et al., 2007). They serve as trusted figures who comprehend the nuances of their congregants' lives, offering a safe space for exploration and healing. Pastoral counseling encompasses various services, including premarital counseling, grief support, and assistance with everyday challenges. While pastoral counselors may not hold formal counseling degrees, their expertise lies in listening actively, offering spiritual insight, and providing compassionate guidance.

In essence, the role of pastors in counseling extends beyond therapy; it integrates faith, compassion, and cultural sensitivity to address the holistic needs of individuals and communities. Their approach is grounded in a commitment to spiritual guidance and personal growth, making them invaluable sources of support and wisdom within their congregations. As pastors navigate the complexities of modern life, they uphold the longstanding tradition of the Black church as a sanctuary for spiritual renewal, community empowerment, and social justice. This legacy ensures that their impact endures across generations, fostering resilience and healing in the face of adversity.

Historically the Black church has been a cornerstone of African American communities and has played a pivotal role in providing spiritual nourishment and practical support to its members. Pastors within this context not only minister to the spiritual needs of their congregants but also serve as advocates for social change and stewards of cultural heritage. The church has been a beacon of hope and resilience during systemic oppression, offering solace and strength through faith and community solidarity.

Moreover, pastoral counseling embodies principles of care that resonate deeply within African American cultural traditions. It emphasizes the importance of communal support, resilience in the face of adversity, and the integration of faith into everyday life. This approach addresses immediate concerns and fosters long-term personal development and community cohesion.

In today's society, where mental health issues are increasingly recognized and addressed, the role of pastors in counseling remains pivotal. They bridge the gap between spiritual guidance and psychological support, offering a holistic approach to healing that acknowledges the interconnectedness of mind, body, and spirit. By integrating psychological insights with spiritual wisdom, pastors create a therapeutic environment that supports personal growth and empowers individuals to overcome challenges with resilience and hope.

Pastoral Counseling

Pastoral counseling is particularly effective in addressing moral dilemmas and existential questions that may not be fully addressed in secular therapeutic settings. It provides a framework for individuals to explore their values, beliefs, and life choices within the context of their faith tradition. This integration of spiritual and psychological dimensions encourages individuals to find meaning and purpose in their experiences, fostering a sense of identity and belonging within their religious community (Neighbors, 1985; Neighbors et al., 1998).

Furthermore, pastoral counselors often engage in ongoing education and training to enhance their skills and effectiveness. While they may not possess formal academic degrees in counseling, their commitment to professional development ensures they provide competent and ethical care to those they serve. This dedication underscores their role as trusted advisors and mentors within their congregations, guiding individuals through life's challenges with empathy, wisdom, and spiritual insight.

Another significant advantage of pastoral counseling is its accessibility, particularly in communities where access to mental health services may be limited. Pastors are often readily available to provide support and guidance during times of crisis or personal difficulty. Their presence within the community fosters a sense of trust and familiarity, making it easier for individuals to seek help without stigma or hesitation (Neighbors, Musick, & Williams, 1998).

The role of pastors in counseling is multifaceted and deeply rooted in a tradition of faith, resilience, and community solidarity. They serve as spiritual leaders, mentors, and counselors, offering a unique blend of spiritual wisdom and psychological support to individuals and families in need. Their contributions extend beyond church walls , influencing social change, promoting mental health awareness, and advocating for justice within their communities.

As pastors continue to navigate the evolving landscape of mental health care, their role remains indispensable in promoting holistic well-being and empowering individuals to live fulfilling and purposeful lives. Pastors uphold the values of compassion, integrity, and social responsibility that define their ministry, through their dedication to pastoral counseling. They ensure that the legacy of the Black church as a sanctuary for spiritual renewal and community empowerment endures, enriching the lives of countless individuals and shaping the future of their communities for generations to come.

Chapter 6: Value of Spiritual or Religious Coping

What is the meaning of the term spirituality? In a 2006 article Sally Hage asserted, "The word *spirituality* is derived from the Latin s*piritus*, meaning breath or life force. Spirituality generally refers to meaning and purpose in one's life, a search for wholeness, and a relationship with a transcendent being" (p. 303). Other authors have also described spirituality as a central aspect of individuals' lives. Swindle (n.d.) wrote, "Spirituality and religion—and all the issues that accompany these, like prayer—are major aspects to many peoples' lives" (p. 8). Spirituality may even be part of one's cultural identity. Throughout the U.S., many people of faith even consider spirituality or religion a part of their race and cultural identity that informs their worldview and sense of self (Sue & Sue, 2011).

In his article "Continuity and Change in the Life Story: A Longitudinal Study of Autobiographical Memories in Emerging Adulthood," Dan McAdams (2006) also described his life-story theory of human identity, which argued that emerging adults provide their lives with a sense of unity and purpose by constructing and internalizing self-defining life stories. People explain who they are, how they came to be, and where they believe their lives may go by formulating, telling, and revising stories about their past and the imagined future (Bruner, 1990).

There has been no more excellent verification of this than in the stories of three parents in my congregation that I recounted in chapter 1. Within one year, two mothers and one father experienced the tragic deaths of their sons. As I tried to be with each of them, it was a terrible drain on the Church and me as pastor. There is something unnatural about parents burying their children. Pastors are expected to bury the old, not the young. I have walked with each of these parents as they have struggled to deal with their tragic loss. Sometimes, I did not know what to say, but I was always ready to listen. As McAdams' article suggested, my greatest service was listening to the parents tell their stories. In retelling their narratives and engaging in prayer and counseling, these parents began to engage in life again. Even when people go through terrible situations, they can come to know and make sense of their lives and know God differently. For believing individuals whose lives have been affected by violence and victimization, religion can offer a source of meaning by considering forgiveness and changing one's mindset to address feeling helpless, hopeless or needing to be in control. People may find comfort in understanding that God's Word can only challenge and overcome one's concerns. Our relationship with and reliance upon God requires that we obey His Word and reveal His wisdom in how we live and love others.

Spirituality and religious coping can offer a source of meaning and resilience for individuals affected by violence and victimization. Believers may find comfort in forgiveness, surrendering control, and trusting God's wisdom and guidance. The practice of faith can provide a framework for processing trauma, fostering inner strength, and promoting a sense of connection with others and with the Lord. In conclusion, spirituality and religious coping play a significant role in navigating the aftermath of urban violence and trauma. By drawing upon spiritual beliefs and practices, individuals can find solace, meaning, and resilience as they confront life's most challenging experiences.

The following scripture references can be used when counseling.

Forgiveness

Matthew 18:21-22 - Then Peter came up and said to him, "Lord, how often will my brother sin against me, and I forgive him? As many as seven times?" Jesus said to him, "I do not say to you seven times, but seventy-seven times.

Matthew 6:14-15 - For if you forgive others their trespasses, your heavenly Father will also forgive you, but if you do not forgive others their trespasses, neither will your Father forgive your trespasses.

Hurt

Isaiah 30:20-21-And though the Lord gives you the bread of adversity and the water of affliction, yet your Teacher will not hide himself anymore, but your eyes shall see your Teacher. And your ears shall hear a word behind you, saying, "This is the way, walk in it," when you turn to the right or when you turn to the left.

1 Peter 5:10- And after you have suffered a little while, the God of all grace, who has called you to his eternal glory in Christ, will himself restore, confirm, strengthen, and establish you.

Trust

Isaiah 41:10- Fear you not; for I am with you: be not dismayed; for I am your God: I will strengthen you; yes, I will help you; yes, I will uphold you with the right hand of My righteousness.

Proverbs 3:5–6- Trust in the LORD with all your heart; and lean not to your own understanding. In all your ways acknowledge Him, and He shall direct your paths.

Hope

Isaiah 40:31 - But those who hope in the LORD will renew their strength. They will soar on wings like eagles; they will run and not grow weary, they will walk and not be faint.

Romans 5:3-4 - Not only so, but we also glory in our sufferings, because we know that suffering produces perseverance; perseverance, character; and character, hope.

As we come to the end of Chapter 7, you've gained valuable insights into the principles and practices that underpin a transformative journey toward restoration. But understanding the concepts is just the beginning. To truly apply these teachings in your life or in the lives of others, you need practical tools and real-world examples that illustrate these principles in action.

That's where the companion book, RESTORE: Practical Insights and Applications, comes in. This valuable resource offers a collection of detailed case studies that bring the theoretical aspects of nouthetic counseling to life. You'll find compelling examples that show how these principles work in various situations, offering you a clearer understanding of how to apply them in real-life scenarios.

In addition, the companion book includes affirmations specifically designed to support those who are navigating their own journeys of healing and growth. These affirmations are crafted to reinforce the teachings from RESTORE and provide encouragement and strength in moments of challenge.

Moreover, you'll discover a curated list of scripture readings that complement each case study and affirmation, helping to deepen your reflection and spiritual growth. These readings are chosen to support and enhance your journey, offering divine guidance and encouragement as you move forward.

Whether you're looking to apply these insights in your personal life, support someone else, or enrich your counseling practice, RESTORE: Practical Insights and Applications is the perfect next step. By integrating these additional resources, you'll gain a more comprehensive understanding and practical tools to truly experience and facilitate restoration.

I invite you to continue your journey of growth and healing by exploring this companion book. Your path to restoration doesn't end here—it's just beginning.

Chapter 7: Nouthetic Counseling

Nouthetic counseling is in a league of its own. Not recognized by the professional counseling community until the 1970s, nouthetic counseling vastly differs from other schools of counseling in that it holds the Word of God as the only objective standard of truth. Nouthetic and Christian counseling are often thought to be the same, however, although all nouthetic counseling is "Christian counseling" (consistent with the teachings of Christ), not all Christian counseling is nouthetic. In cases of trauma, secular psychology looks for what may have caused a depressive episode, anxiety, or a particular phobia. Nouthetic counseling relies on a biblical approach and application to every situation. To this end, any counselor who does not fully subscribe to biblically based Christ-centered counseling cannot be legitimately labeled a nouthetic counselor. Dohose (2009) suggested in "Paul's Passing Thoughts: The Role of Counseling in the Church" the need to embrace the biblical model of nouthetic counseling: "If we are to be a healing community that glorifies God, counseling from the scriptures must be returned to its lofty position in the church for it plays a major role in sanctification and discipleship" (para. 7).

The founder of nouthetic counseling, Dr. Jay Adams (2009) wrote that it starts with Christ and ends with Christ when the client acknowledges and repents his or her sin, thus resolving the problem. He goes on to state, "In Nouthetic Counseling, clients are taught to solve problems rather than adapt to them. There is a biblical solution to every problem" (Adams, 2009, p. 130).

Biblically Based

Nouthetic counseling is biblically based—the Word of God is supreme. It rejects secular treatment and avoids any digression from a biblical basis. It can also occur anywhere, no matter the counselor's vocation(Culbertson, 2009). Those who are pure nouthetic counselors believe the Bible is the only foundation to be used in counseling, although this may not be easy. Eigelbach (2006) wrote:

> *"People have helped people for years armed with no other tool than their Bibles. This is the premise of the AACC philosophy, Caring for People God's Way. Unlike secular counselors, nouthetic counselors see people as naturally prone toward wrongdoing and error, unable to help themselves no matter how they can see their problem. Helping them takes more than naming a problem and shooting it down with a Bible verse. "(p. 5)*

Believers in nouthetic counseling proclaim that the power of the Holy Spirit is sufficient to equip Christian counselors to assist their clients in restoring broken relationships and providing them with a sense of empowerment.

Personality change in Scripture involves confession, repentance, and the development of new biblical patterns. None of this is viewed legalistically, but all must be understood as the work of the Holy Spirit. Nouthetic confrontation involves the verbal ministry of the Word. All such ministry is made effectual by the power of the Spirit alone. (Adams, 2009, Kindle Location, 4171) Adams (2009) wrote: "Counseling is the work of the Holy Spirit. Effective counseling cannot be done apart from him. He is called the paraclete "counselor." Instead of depending on years of secular therapeutic techniques, the counselee is expected to change—by the power of the Holy Spirit as he begins to meet the requirements identified in Romans 8:28-29. (p. 20)

No academic or professional credentials are required to be a nouthetic counselor. The only prerequisite is to demonstrate solid biblical foundations rooted in prayer and understanding biblical principles. These will fully qualify an individual to meet the challenges of religiously minded clients, whether male or female, including those representing a wide range of ethnicities, denominational backgrounds, and socioeconomic statuses.

Education and Training

Some Christians believe that there are errors in integrating secular thought with the Bible and have preferred biblical (nouthetic) counseling even to standard Christian counseling programs. Colossians 2:8 says, "Beware lest anyone cheat you through philosophy and empty deceit, according to the tradition of men, according to the basic principles of the world, and not according to Christ" (NKJV). Eareckson-Tada (n.d.) said:

> *"I have spent the more significant part of my ministry defending the inerrancy, authority, and sufficiency of the Word of God. There was a time when this defense was necessary only against those outside the Church. Today, sadly, many who claim to be within orthodox Christianity have abandoned a firm stand on Scripture. This tragedy is seen in all aspects of church ministry, but most readily regarding counseling. Instead of running to the one source that provides answers for heart issues--Christ and His Word--church leaders have become enamored with*

> *psychology and worldly philosophy. The need today, therefore, is a return to and a proclamation of clear biblical truth within evangelicalism. I am encouraged to hear of the formation of the Association of Biblical Counselors. This new organization is committed to true biblical counseling. Their efforts to promote biblical ministry, along with the resources they will provide and the fellowship they will foster, are a welcome addition to the battle to guard the truth that has been entrusted to us." (para. 1)*

There are few colleges and seminaries that teach nouthetic counseling. However, during the 2005 Convention of the Southern Baptist Theological Seminary, it was announced that the Louisville School, the seminary's flagship school, would no longer participate in the Clinical Pastoral Education Program and offer pastoral counseling but would instead provide biblical counseling. Biblical counseling is now taught in all of the Southern Baptist Church Seminaries. In a 2007 article, Winfrey wrote: "It was not a big surprise in 2005 when Southern Baptist Theological Seminary announced that it was making a "wholesale change" in its counseling program. The Louisville School…declared that it was jettisoning the 'pastoral counseling' model [which attempted to integrate psychology with biblical principles] in favor of 'biblical counseling' [a purely biblical approach] (para. 1)." Scott (n.d.) also expressed approval that a new group of counselors, the Association of Biblical Counselors, would support counseling based on the word of God. Scott stated:

> *"I am blessed to be a part of an institution (Southern Seminary) that is seeking to be faithful to God's Word in*

the area of counseling. I am also excited to be associated with another group (Association of Biblical Counselors) coming on the scene that will stand and labor for the authority and sufficiency of God's Word. For many years, the call to counsel biblically fought to be heard. Today, amongst the still confused state of even Christian counseling, God's people have an increasing desire to find discipleship/counselors who do not compromise His Word. There are more and more opportunities to provide what is needed to assist the Church in establishing a solid foundation and counseling ministry. The Association of Biblical Counselors will no doubt be a great vehicle to do just that. May God's richest blessings be upon this association as it seeks to remain faithful to God, His Word, and its ministry to His people." (para. 1)

Godsey (2004) went on to examine the effectiveness and the use of nouthetic counseling among Black Southern Baptist pastors in the Baltimore Baptist Association. Godsey devised and mailed questionnaires to eighteen African American Southern Baptist pastors in an effort to examine the effectiveness and use of nouthetic counseling. The responses were analyzed through a qualitative study, and a minimal quantitative study was provided to help understand the qualitative data. The author was able to compare several psychotherapeutic styles that involve "lovingly confronting people through the word of God to face their counseling issues and help make the changes needed." The author also acknowledged differences in biblical-based counseling now as opposed to decades ago when Jay Adams first launched nouthetic counseling.

Critique of Nouthetic Counseling

Admittedly, nouthetic counseling may not be for everyone. White (1985) thought extensive use of Scripture might be inappropriate in many situations and might seem judgmental moralism. Some may be wounded by nouthetic counseling, not only being unable to change or worse off than before but carrying the added weight of believing they experienced failure because they did not pray hard enough, read long enough, or have enough faith to deal with their anorexic behavior, bulimia, depression, and other types of anxieties. Biblical counseling may also cause dependency on the specialist and be oppressive for women. Women may be told that the biblical mandate is for them to stay married and to be submissive to their husbands, even in cases of spousal abuse. This writer acknowledges that some nouthetic practitioners may have abused their authority and misrepresented or misinterpreted Scripture, causing harm to their clients. However, similar problems may be found within traditional therapeutic settings. The evidence still shows there are a vast number of people seeking counselors, therapists, and psychiatrists who are Christian or who demonstrate a Judeo-Christian faith base.

Benefits For Trauma Survivors

1. Spiritual Perspective: Nouthetic counseling incorporates a spiritual perspective, helping trauma survivors find meaning, hope, and comfort in their faith. By exploring biblical truths and principles, individuals may gain insight into their suffering and find solace in believing God is present in their pain and can bring healing and redemption.

2. Emotional Support: Nouthetic counselors provide a safe and supportive environment for trauma survivors to express their feelings, fears, and

struggles. Through compassionate listening and empathetic understanding, counselors can validate survivors' experiences and offer emotional support grounded in biblical truths.

3. Integration of Faith and Healing: Nouthetic counseling seeks to integrate faith and healing, recognizing the interconnectedness of spiritual, emotional, and psychological well-being. Counselors may help trauma survivors explore how their faith can inform their healing journey, offering guidance on forgiveness, reconciliation, and finding purpose amid suffering.

4. Scripture-Based Coping Strategies: Nouthetic counseling equips trauma survivors with practical coping strategies rooted in Scripture, such as prayer, meditation on God's Word, and reliance on the power of prayer. By drawing on biblical wisdom and guidance, individuals can develop resilience and strength to navigate the challenges of trauma recovery.

5. Addressing Root Issues: Nouthetic counseling seeks to address underlying heart issues that may contribute to trauma symptoms, such as unforgiveness, bitterness, or unresolved conflicts. By examining these issues in light of biblical truth, individuals can experience freedom from emotional bondage and find healing from past hurts.

6. Holistic Approach: Nouthetic counseling takes a holistic approach to healing, addressing the spiritual, emotional, and relational aspects of trauma recovery. Counselors may work collaboratively with trauma survivors to identify areas of struggle and develop personalized plans for growth and healing that encompass all dimensions of their lives.

As people of God, we are called to be beacons of hope in a world often overshadowed by darkness. We are instruments in the hands of the Most

High, vessels through which His love and light can shine forth. Our role in counseling is not merely to offer temporary solutions or bandage wounds but to extend the Gospel's transformative power – a message of healing, deliverance, and the unending love of God.

In our journey as counselors, we recognize that we are not the ultimate healers but conduits through which the divine healing presence flows. Through our words, actions, and prayers individuals can experience the profound restoration promised by God. As stated in 1 Peter 5:10, "And the God of all grace, who called you to his eternal glory in Christ, after you have suffered a little while, will himself restore you and make you strong, firm and steadfast."

This verse reminds us that suffering is not the end of the story. In the hands of a loving God, suffering catalyzes transformation and renewal. Through our counseling ministry, we have the privilege of witnessing God's redemptive work in the lives of those who have endured pain and hardship. We stand as witnesses to His faithfulness, compassion, and promise to bring beauty out of ashes.

Our role as counselors extends beyond merely alleviating symptoms; it encompasses the holistic restoration of individuals – body, mind, and Spirit. We recognize that true healing comes from encountering the presence of God, who is the source of all restoration and wholeness. Our task is to create an environment where individuals can encounter the transformative power of God's love, where wounds can be healed, chains can be broken, and lives can be restored.

As we journey alongside those who are hurting, we do so with the assurance that we are partnering with the Divine Healer Himself. Our faith is not in our own abilities or expertise, but in the promise of God to work all things together for good for those who love Him (Romans 8:28). With each counseling session, we are privileged to witness God's grace at work, bringing hope, healing, and transformation to those who are in darkness.

As counselors, we have been entrusted with a sacred task – to be vessels of God's healing and restoration in a broken world. Let us never underestimate the power of our role or the impact of our ministry. Through our words, prayers, and actions, may we continue to spread the Gospel of hope and healing, bringing light to those who walk in darkness and pointing them to the One who is the ultimate source of restoration and redemption.

FINAL THOUGHTS

As pastors and counselors, we are entrusted with the sacred mission of guiding individuals through their journey of restoration from trauma—a mission that is both a profound privilege and a significant responsibility. Trauma can leave deep, invisible scars that permeate every aspect of a person's life—emotional, spiritual, and physical. Our role is to walk beside them in their pain, to offer them the hope and healing found in Christ, and to help them discover a peace that transcends understanding.

In my own experience, nouthetic counseling is an incredibly powerful tool in this restorative process. This method, deeply rooted in the Greek concept of "nouthesia," or admonishment and instruction, is not just about confronting individuals' struggles. It's about lovingly guiding them back to the truth of Scripture, which offers the only true solutions to the brokenness they face. Nouthetic counseling is founded on the belief that God's Word is sufficient for all matters of life and faith, and through it, genuine change and healing can occur.

What makes this process so uniquely transformative is the essential role of the Holy Spirit. The Holy Spirit is not just a participant in the counseling process; He is the foundation upon which it rests. He reveals the hidden wounds, the deep-rooted issues that often lie beneath the surface of trauma. As counselors our task is to remain sensitive to His leading and to ensure that our counsel is not based on human wisdom alone but on the divine insight and compassion that only the Holy Spirit can provide.

When we place our trust in the Holy Spirit, we can address trauma in a way that goes far beyond mere psychological techniques. He gives us the discernment to see what is often hidden and to minister to the whole person—emotionally, psychologically, and spiritually. This kind of spiritual sensitivity is what allows us to bring true healing, to help those we counsel not just to manage their pain but to find true freedom and restoration in Christ.

As you continue in your ministry, I encourage you to fully embrace this God-given healing process through nouthetic counseling. Believe in the power of God's Word, trust in the guidance of the Holy Spirit, and remain steadfast in your commitment to lovingly confront and counsel those in need. The journey may be challenging, but the rewards are eternal—seeing lives transformed, hearts healed, and faith renewed.

Remember, our work is not merely about addressing problems—it's about facilitating encounters with the living God, who alone can heal the deepest wounds. As Romans 15:13 says, "May the God of hope fill you with all joy and peace in believing, so that by the power of the Holy Spirit you may abound in hope." Let this be the cornerstone of your counseling ministry, knowing that through the power of the Holy Spirit, you are helping to bring about genuine healing and lasting peace in the lives of those you serve.

May you continue to walk this path with courage, compassion, and an unwavering faith in the transformative power of God's Word.

Blessings on your journey!

BIBLIOGRAPHY

Adams, J. (1973). The Christian Counselor's Manual. Grand Rapids, MI: Zondervan.

Adams, J. E. (2009). Competent to counsel: Introduction to nouthetic counseling (Jay Adams Library). Zondervan. Kindle Edition.

Aten, J. D., Topping, S., Denney, R. M., & Bayne, T. G. (2010). Collaborating with African American churches to overcome minority disaster mental health disparities: What mental health professionals can learn from Hurricane Katrina. Professional Psychology: Research and Practice, 41(2), 167-173. doi:http://dx.doi.org/10.1037/a0018116

Biblical counselors have continued to believe that any positive change must flow from the power of Christ as he does his work in the believer through the power of the Holy Spirit. All Lambert, Heath (2011-11-02).

The Biblical Counseling Movement after Adams (Foreword by David Powlison) (p. 45). Crossway. Kindle Edition.

Boston violent crime dives to 31-year low (2002). Crime Control Digest, 36(36), 3.

Bruner, J. (1990). Acts of meaning. Cambridge, MA: Harvard University Press.

Brushwyler, R. L, Fancher, S. C., Matthews, J. R. & Stone, M. M. R. (1999). Pastoral care vs. professional counseling: Discerning the differences. Retrieved from http://www.ipcaworldwide.org/resources/Articles/ CareVsCoun.pdf

Campbell, A. (1987). Self-definition by rejection: The case of gang girls. Social Problems, 34(5), 451-466. Retrieved from http://search.proquest.com/docview/617513348?accountid=34899

Campbell, A. (1991). The girls in the gang. Boston, MA: Basil Blackwell Inc.

Cantave, A. (2007). Crime in the African-American neighborhood: A report of the Trotter roundtable on crime. Retrieved from http://scholarworks.umb.edu/ cgi/viewcontent.cgi?article=1000&context=trotter_pubs

Carrasco, V. (1999). Female gang participation: Causes and solutions. Retrieved from https://web.stanford.edu/class/e297c/poverty_prejudice/ganginterv/hfemalegang.htm

Collins, G. R. (1988). Christian counseling: A comprehensive guide (rev. ed.).

Dallas, TX: Word Books.

Comas-Díaz, L. (2011). Multicultural care: A clinician's guide to cultural competence. Washington, DC: American Psychological Association.

Constantine, M. G., Wilton, L., Gainor, K. A., & Lewis, E. L. (2002). Religious participation, spirituality, and coping among African American college students. Journal of College Student Development, 43(5), 605.

Creswell, John W. (2012-03-13). Qualitative Inquiry and Research Design: Choosing Among Five Approaches (Kindle Locations 3471-3473). SAGE Publications. Kindle Edition

d'Entremont, C. (2012). Forgotten youth: Re-engaging students through dropout recovery. Retrieved from http://www.renniecenter.org/research/ ForgottenYouth.pdf

Dersch, C. A. (2002). Therapist reactions to treating cases of partner violence. Retrieved from ProQuest Dissertations & Theses: Full Text database. (UMI No. 3056067)

Dohose, P. (2009). Paul's passing thoughts: The role of counseling in the church. Retrieved from http://paulspassingthoughts.com/2009/09/04/the role-of-counseling-in-the-church/

Eareckson-Tada, J. (n.d.). Association of Biblical Counselors. Retrieved from http://christiancounseling.com/content/endorsements

Eigelbach, K. (2006, November 21). Seeking counsel in the bible. Cincinnati Post, p. 5.

Falaye, A. O. (2013). Counseling from the Christian point of view. IFE Psychologia: An International Journal, 21(3), 80-91.

Gillham, B. (n.d.). What is Christian counseling? Retrieved from http://www.cftministry. org/counseling/what_is_christian_counseling.htm

Godsey, A. E. (2004). Nouthetic counseling and its usage in the pastorate of black American Baptist pastors of the Baltimore Baptist Association located in Baltimore, Maryland (Unpublished doctoral dissertation). Capella University, Minneapolis, MN.

Green, L. (2015). Pastoral nouthetic counseling for urban residents dealing with trauma resulting from violence: A doctoral dissertation research proposal (Doctoral dissertation). Argosy University, Phoenix Campus.Hage, S. (2006). A closer look at the role of spirituality in psychology training programs. Professional Psychology: Research and Practice, 37(3), 303-310.

Hall, S. A., & Gjesfjeld, C. D. (2013). Clergy: A partner in rural mental health? Journal of Rural Mental Health, 37(1), 50-57. doi:http://dx.doi.org/10.1037/rmh0000006

Harris, M. G. (1998). Cholas: Latino girls and gangs. New York, NY: AMS Press.

Homicides in Boston reach 5-year high (2001). Crime Control Digest, 35(41), 2.

Humes, E. (1997). No matter how loud I shout: A year in the life of juvenile court. New York, NY: First Touchstone.

Jones, P. (2006). Biblical counseling vs. secular counseling. Retrieved from http://www.dovechristiancounseling.com/Biblical-Counseling-vs-Secular Counseling.html

Jordan, J. (2004). Crime reduction Boston Police Department's winning plan. Journal of California Law Enforcement, 38(2), 13-16.

Kollar, C. (1997). Solution-focused pastoral counseling: An-effective short term approach to getting people back on track. Grand Rapids, MI: Zondervan. Koss, M. P., & Shiang, J. (1994). Research on brief psychotherapy. In A. E. Bergin & S. L. Garfield (Eds.), Handbook of psychotherapy and behavior change (4th ed., pp. 664–700). New York, NY: Wiley

Kreger, A. (2011). Nouthetic counseling: a Biblical approach or solving emotional problems Retrieved from port by African Americans: A focus group study. American Journal of Orthopsychiatry, 77(2), 249-258.

McAdams, D. (2006). Continuity and change in the life story: A longitudinal study of autobiographical memories in emerging adulthood. Journal of Personality; 74(5), 1371-1400.

McMinn, M. R., Ruiz, J. N., Marx, D., Wright, J. B., & Gilbert, N. B. (2006). Professional psychology and the doctrines of sin awww.ibcd.org/aboutusnou.html

Lambert, H. (2012). The biblical counseling movement after Adams. Retrieved from http://www.ccef.org/sites/default/files/journal-articles/the_biblical_counseling_movement_after_adams_smith.pdf

La Roche, M., & Tawa, J. (2011). Taking back our streets: A clinical model for empowering urban youths through participation in peace promotion. Peace and

Conflict: Journal of Peace Psychology, 17(1), 4-21. doi:10.1080/10781911003769165

La Torre, M. A. (2004). Prayer in psychotherapy: An important consideration. Perspectives in Psychiatric Care, 40(1), 2-40.

MacArthur, J. F., Jr., & Mack, W. A. (1994). Introduction to Biblical counseling: A basic guide to the principles and practice of counseling. Nashville, TN: W. Publishing Group.

Marks, L., Nesteruk, O., Swanson, M., Garrison, B., & Davis, T. (2005). Religion and health among African Americans: A qualitative examination. Research on Aging, 27(4), 447-474. doi:http://dx.doi.org/10.1177/0164027505276252

Rowell Huesmann, L., Moise-Titus, J., Podolski, C.-L., Eron, L. D. (2003). Longitudinal relations between children's exposure to TV violence and their aggressive and violent behavior in young adulthood: 1977-1992. Developmental Psychology, 39(2), 201-221. Mattis, J. S., Mitchell, N., Zapata, A., Grayman, N. A., Taylor, R. J. & Chatters, L. M. (2007). Uses of ministerial supnd grace: Christian leaders' perspectives. Professional Psychology: Research and Practice, 37(3), 295-295-302. doi:10.1037/0735-7028.37.3.295

McMinn, M. R., Staley, R. C., Webb, K. C., & Seegobin, W. (2010). Just what is Christian counseling anyway? Professional Psychology: Research and Practice, 41(5), 391-391-397. doi:10.1037/a0018584

Miles, C. A. (1913). In the garden. Retrieved from http://www.hymnsite.com/lyrics/umh314.sht

Milevsky, A., & Eisenberg, M. (2012). Spiritually oriented treatment with Jewish clients: Meditative prayer and religious texts. Professional Psychology: Research and Practice, 43(4), 336-340. doi:http://dx.doi.org/10.1037/a0028035

Neale, G. A. (2011). Straight talk on getting there. Retrieved from http://www.lulu.com/shop/george-neale/straight-talk-on-getting-there/paperback/product-1159547.html

Neighbors, H. W., Musick, M. A., & Williams, D. R. (1998). The African American minister as a source of help for serious personal crises: Bridge or barrier to mental health care? Health Education & Behavior, 25(6), 759-777. doi:http://dx.doi.org/10.1177/109019819802500606.

Patrick, W. (2010). Frequently asked questions (FAQS). Retrieved from http://www.drpaatrick.com/faq.htm

Scott, W. (n.d.). Pastoral counseling notes. Retrieved from http://jcsm.org/Education/Pastoral_Counseling.htm

Scriven, J. (1855). What a friend we have in Jesus! Retrieved from http://library.timelesstruths.org/music/What_a_Friend_We_Have_in_Jesus/

Serofin, A. (2014). Urban violence: War by any other name. Red Cross Red Crescent, 1, 22-26.

Shafranske, E. P., & Malony, H. N. (1996). Religion and the clinical practice of psychology: A case for inclusion. In E. P. Shafranske (Ed.), Religion and the clinical practice of psychology (pp. 561-586). Washington, DC: American Psychological Association.

Shannon, D. K., Oakes, K. E., Scheers, N. J., Richardson, F. J., & Stills, A. B. (2013). Religious beliefs as moderator of exposure to violence in African American adolescents. Psychology of Religion and Spirituality, 5(3), 172-181. doi:10.1037/a0030879.

Simon, C. E., Crowther, M., & Higgerson, H. (2007). The stage-specific role of spirituality among African American Christian women

Solis, A. L. (2009). A case study of bullying and other aggressive interactions among children in a public middle school (Doctoral dissertation). Available from ProQuest Dissertations and Theses. (Accession No. 305172253)

Southern Baptist Convention (2002). Resolution No. 5. On the sufficiency of Scripture In a therapeutic culture. Retrieved from http://www.sbcannualmeeting.net/sbc02/resolutions/default.asp

Sprinkle, R., (2005). Follow me: Becoming a lifestyle prayer walker. Birmingham, AL: New Hope.

Sue, D. W., (2010). Microaggressions in Everyday Life: Race, Gender, and Sexual Orientation (p. 268).

Sue, D. W., & Sue, D. (2011). Counseling the culturally diverse: Theory and practice, (6th ed.). Retrieved from http://online.vitalsource.com/books/

9781118559734.

Swindle, K. L. (n.d.). Using prayer in professional counseling. Retrieved from https:// www.regent.edu/admin/stusrv/writingcenter/files/

Taylor, R. J., & Chatters, L. M. (1986). Church-based informal support among elderly blacks. The Gerontologist, 26(6), 637-642.

Tuggle, M. B. (1995, August). New insights and challenges about churches as intervention sites to reach the African-American community with health information. Journal of the National Medical Association, 87, 635-637.

Vigil, J. D. (1993). Gangs, social control, and ethnicity: Ways to redirect: Report on. identity and inner-city youth. New York, NY: Teachers College

Vigil, J. D. (2003). Urban violence and street gangs. Annual Review of Anthropology, 32(1), 225-242.

Villafane, E. (2006). Beyond cheap grace: A call to radical discipleship, incarnation, and justice. Grand Rapids, MI: Wm. B. Eerdmans Publishing Co.

Walsh, F. (2008). Spiritual resources in family therapy (2nd ed.). New York, NY: Guilford Press (Kindle edition).

Ward, E. C. (2005). Keeping it real: A grounded theory study of African American clients engaging in counseling at a community mental health agency. Journal of Counseling Psychology, 52(4), 471-481. doi:http://dx.doi.org/ 10.1037/0022-0167.52.4.471

Weld, C., & Eriksen, K. (2007). Christian clients' preferences regarding prayer as a counseling intervention. Journal of Psychology and Theology, 35(4), 328-341.

White, R. (1985). A critique of the nouthetic counseling technique of Jay E. Adams. (Unpublished doctoral dissertation). Wilfrid Laurier University, Canada.

Winfrey, D. (2007). Biblical counseling controversy. Retrieved from http://www. dwinfrey.com/portfolio/biblical-counseling/

Winship, C., & Berrien, J. (1999). Boston cops and black churches. Public Interest, 136, 52-68. Retrieved from http://search.proquest.com/docview/222058137? accountid=34899

Zinnbauer, B. J., & Pargament, K. I. (2000). Working with the sacred: Four approaches to religious and spiritual issues in counseling. Journal of Counseling and Development, 78, 162-171. DOI: 10.1002/j.1556-6676.2000.tb02574.x

ABOUT THE AUTHOR

Dr. Larry Green, Ph.D. in Christian Counseling, is a devoted champion of God, His Word, and the extraordinary individuals God created. With over 50 years of extensive experience in ministry, education, and counseling, Dr. Green's life exemplifies unwavering faith and a deep commitment to fostering peace and healing within communities.

Dr. Green's journey began with a Bachelor of Science in Elementary Education, a Master of Education, and later, a Doctor of Education in Pastoral Community Counseling. His passion for guiding and supporting others led him to earn life coaching credentials from the American Association of Christian Counselors (AACC) and Prepare/Enrich Marriage Counselor certification.

For 28 inspiring years, Dr. Green served as the senior pastor at Timothy Baptist Church in Roxbury, Massachusetts, where his compassionate leadership left an indelible mark on the congregation. As Pastor Emeritus, he continues to influence lives through his teachings and writings.

Beyond his pastoral work, Dr. Green is an esteemed Adjunct Professor at the School of the Great Commission Bible College & Seminary. He imparts wisdom as a Professor of New Testament Survey and The Divided Kingdom and as an instructor of Pastoral Nouthetic Counseling. Additionally, he serves as a Counseling Consultant, guiding individuals, organizations, and families through life's complexities.

Dr. Green's dedication to education extended to Boston Public Schools, where he spent 31 years as a teacher and administrator. His leadership also extended to roles such as president of the Baptist Ministers Conference of Boston and Vicinity and State Vice President of the New England Missionary Baptist Convention.

His commitment to community service is evident through his involvement with various boards, including the Brockton Council on Aging, Roxbury Multi-Service Center, METCO, Pine Street Inn, and the Solomon Carter Fuller Mental Health Center. A significant highlight of his ministry includes leading international prayer walks in cities like Madrid, Paris, and Istanbul.

Dr. Green's literary contributions are equally impactful. His publication, "God in Our Right Now," addresses the trauma of urban violence and offers practical counseling and coaching directives. His latest work, "Restore," continues this mission, providing readers with spiritual and emotional restoration tools.

Dr. Green shares his life's journey with his beloved wife, Dr. Betty Ruth Green. Together, they cherish their three children and four grandchildren, drawing joy and inspiration from their family and faith.

For more insights into Dr. Green's journey and resources for personal and spiritual growth, visit www.Godrightnow.net.

www.ingramcontent.com/pod-product-compliance
Lightning Source LLC
LaVergne TN
LVHW020416070526
838199LV00054B/3627